T5-AOB-643

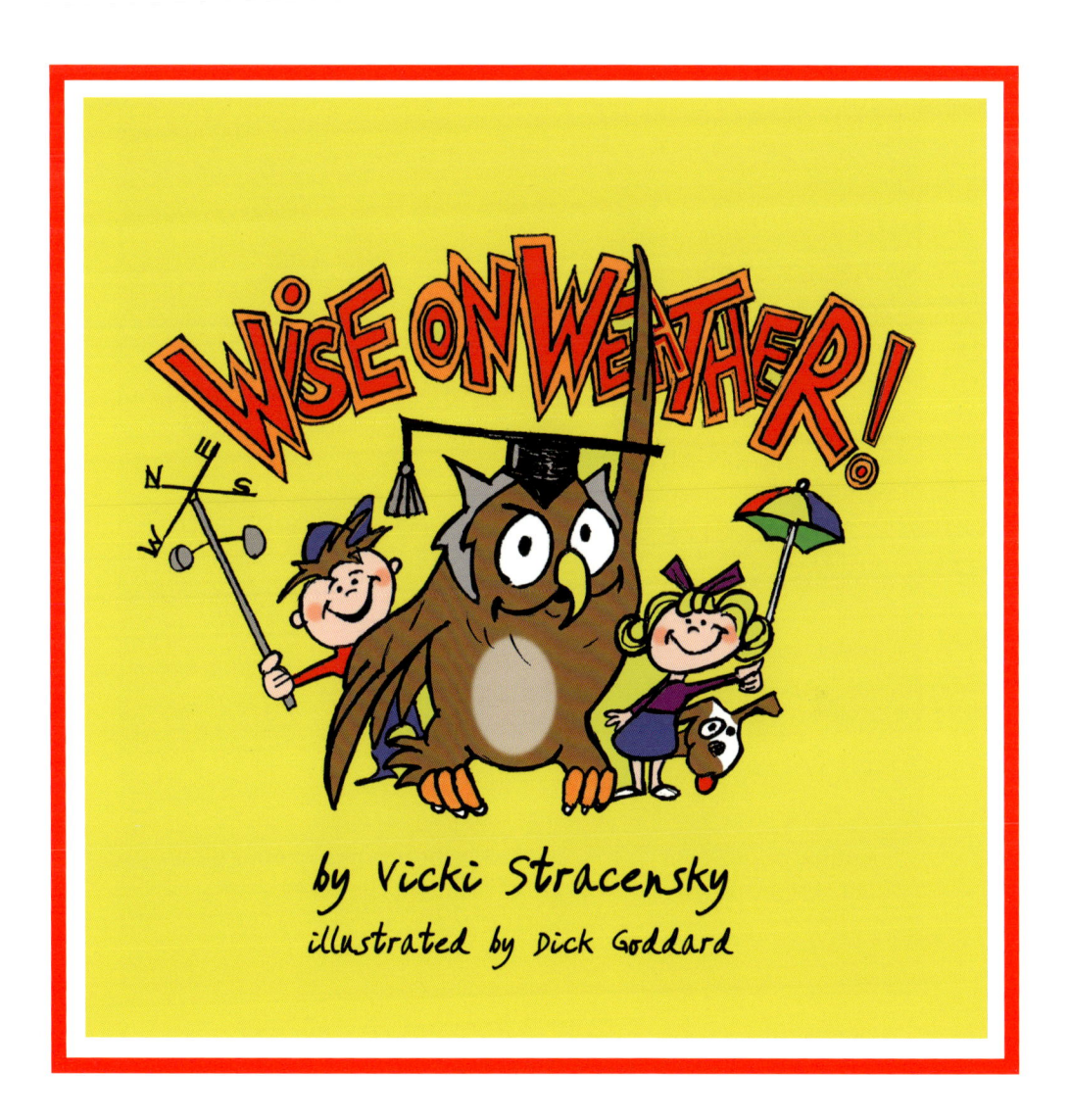

Wise on Weather!

by Vicki Stracensky

illustrated by Dick Goddard

A heartfelt thanks to my husband, children, parents, brothers (Mark, Bryan & David), André Bernier, Dick Goddard, Gorecki family, Bob Levkulich, Bill Martin, Joyce A. McCarthy-Reed, Nemet family, Allison Noga, Jim Stracensky, Jane Toma, Lisa M. Umina, Chris Winslow and Stan Znidarsic. I appreciate all you have done to help this book become a reality. Thank You!

Wise on Weather!
Second Edition, 2015
Wise on Weather! © 2010 Vicki Stracensky
Illustrator: Dick Goddard

All Rights Reserved.
No part of this book may be used or reproduced by any means, graphic, electronic, or mechanical, including photocopying, recording, taping or by any information storage retrieval system now known or hereafter invented, without the written permission of the author/publisher except in the case of brief quotations embodied in critical articles and reviews.

Vicki Stracensky, Author/Publisher
E-mail: vicki@wiseonweather.com
www.wiseonweather.com

Author photo courtesy of stargazerphotography.com
Illustrator photo courtesy of johnashleyphotography.com

Library of Congress Control Number: 2015902798
ISBN 978-0-692-38922-5

Printed in the United States of America

To God: I am here because this is where You want me to be and You know what's best for me. I trust that with You on my side, it will all work out... somehow, someway, someday. Thank You for all of the blessings in my life!

To Matthew, Daniel, Mollie and Evan: My loves, my children, my life. Thank you for praying for me that my dreams would come true. Mommy loves you forever and a day!

To my mother, Barbara: My best friend who has taught me what unconditional love is. If I am half the mother to my four children as you are to your four children, then life will be awesome! Thank you for everything. I love you, Mom!

The weather can be sunny and brighten up your day,

Like someone saying,
"I love you!"
with a beautiful bouquet.

The weather can be cloudy and cover up the sun,

But finding neat designs
in the clouds
can be a lot of fun.

The weather can be foggy, and you can't see very far.
Your parents should be careful when they're driving in the car.

The weather can be rainy. Look out or you'll get wet.

Splashing in puddles can be a blast, especially with your pet.

The weather can be stormy when a hurricane shows its fury.

It's one of nature's most powerful storms, so find safety in a hurry.

The weather can be windy and blow your hat away.
Chasing it down can surely be a fun game to play.

The weather can be unstable.
Take cover down below.
Twisters can be dangerous,
so safety you should know.

The weather can be electric. Lightning fills the sky.

When these bolts keep happening, it looks like the Fourth of July.

The weather can be snowy. Brrr, it will be cold.
Snowballs, snowmen, and sledding are fun for young and old.

Whether you like summer or whether you like spring,

Enjoying Mother Nature can be a wonderful thing.

Whether you like winter or whether you like fall,
Go outside to play and you can really have a ball.

Winter, spring, summer, or fall,
You can have a favorite
or like them all.

When you put these
four seasons together,
Your experiences
can make you
"Wise on Weather!"

WOW!

SEASONAL SAFETY

Every season offers great experiences and many fun things to do. However, every season also contains dangers of which you need to be aware.

WOO (Wise Old Owl) wants you to know seasonal safety. By learning and practicing good safety, you and your loved ones will become "Wise on Weather!" and can enjoy all the beauty and fun Mother Nature has to offer in every season.

FALL

Wear sunglasses when it is windy so that objects do not fly into your eyes.
Be careful while playing outside because leaves can be very slippery.
Make sure the leaf piles you play in have no debris, so you do not get hurt when you jump in.
Do not play in leaf piles near the street because drivers cannot see you.
It gets dark outside earlier, so stay close to home.

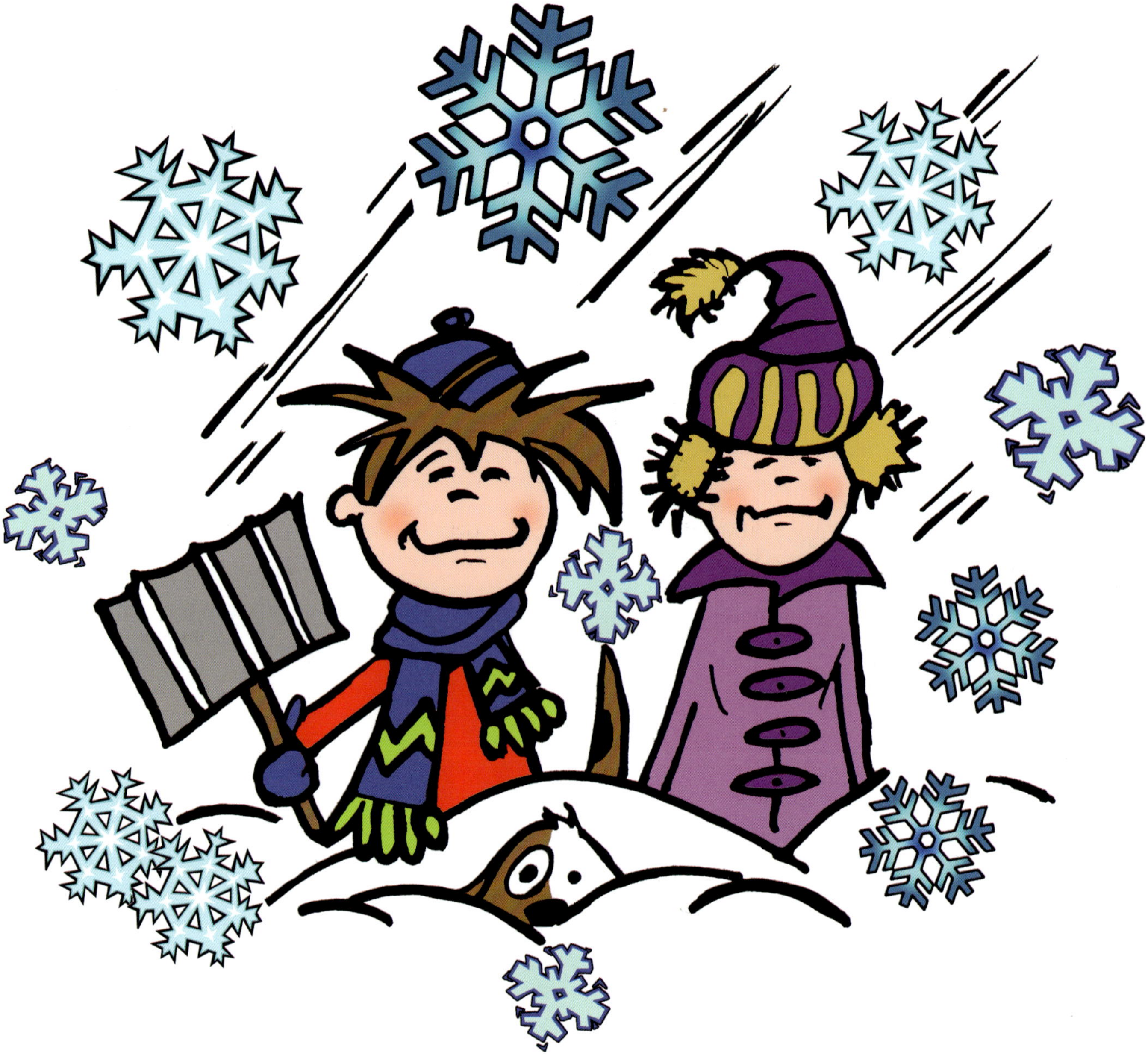

WINTER

Do not eat snow. It is the atmosphere's vacuum cleaner.

Dress warmly and in layers so that you do not get
hypothermia – a dangerous drop in body temperature.

Always wear a hat when outside. You lose a lot of heat from your head.

Wear waterproof boots and gloves and cover your skin so it is not exposed to
the elements, which can give you frostbite – a freezing of the skin.

Provide food and shelter for pets and help the elderly by shoveling their snow.

Clear away snow from around fire hydrants. In case there is a fire,
the firefighters can do their jobs without interruption.

Do not play where icicles are hanging. They can fall down and hurt you.

Ice can be deceiving and dangerous. Be careful that you do not slip and fall
because you can hurt yourself. NO ICE IS SAFE ICE!
The only ice you should play on is at a skating rink.

Do not play on snow piles near the street because drivers cannot see you.

Be aware that snow can collapse. Be careful when you are
digging in the snow and building snow forts.

Always use the buddy system when playing. If something happens to you,
your buddy can help you or go to get help.

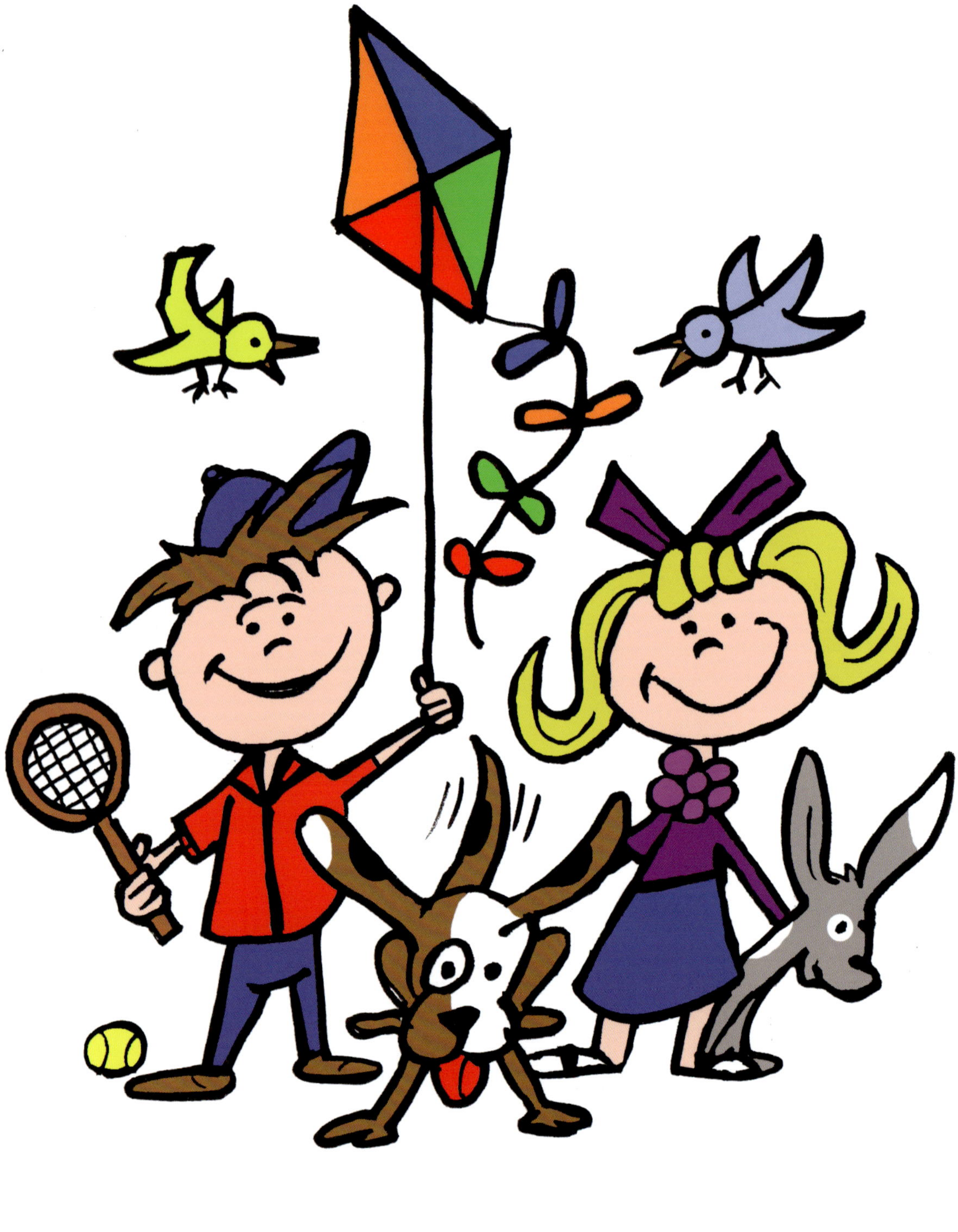

SPRING

Ask your parents to buy a weather radio so you know when storms are coming.

Stay inside during a storm if you can, and do not use the telephone
or television – except in an emergency.

During storms, stay away from beaches and out of pools because water is a
great conductor of electricity. Do not take a shower or bath either.

NEVER touch downed power lines or wires!

Do not hold golf clubs, aluminum baseball bats, umbrellas, or fishing rods during a storm.

If lightning is spotted, you should stop play immediately and take cover. You should not
resume play again until at least a half hour from the last sighting of lightning.

Take tornado watches and warnings very seriously. If you ever hear a loud sound
like a roaring train, take cover immediately.

Go to the lowest area of your house (preferably a basement) away from doors and windows.

Tuck down on your knees in the "tornado drill" position and cover as much of the back
of your head as you can with your arms to protect against flying debris.

If you are stuck outside, get into the "tornado drill" position and do not lie flat.
Do not stand on a hilltop, under a tall or isolated tree, or out in wide open fields.

Move to higher ground immediately during a flood.

Do not try to walk through flooded areas because it takes as little as six inches of
moving water to knock you over.

Floodwaters can be contaminated, so do not play in them.

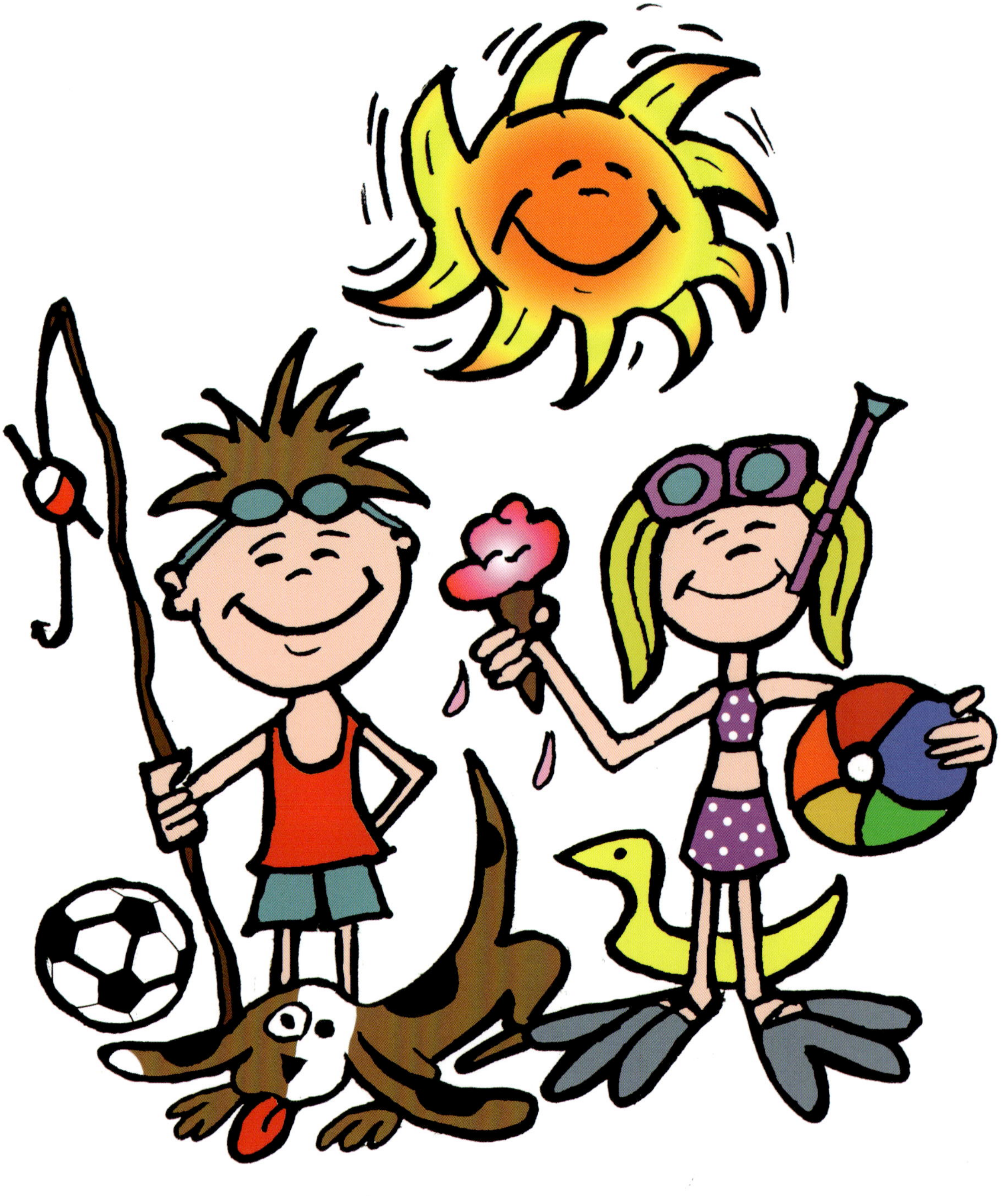

SUMMER

Wear lightweight, light-colored clothing.
Do not let your body get overheated because you can get heatstroke –
a dangerous condition where the body temperature becomes abnormally elevated.

Parents should not leave their children or animals in a car because the temperature
inside the car can get so much hotter than what it is outside.
This can cause dehydration – even death.

Drink plenty of water whenever you are outdoors in the heat.

If you are in the sun, make sure you put on sunscreen and reapply it often
so you do not get sunburn. You should do this all year round when there is sun
because it is the rays of the sun, not the temperature, that cause skin damage.

Make sure you protect your eyes and wear sunglasses outside.
Try not to look directly into the sun.

Learn how to swim and practice good safety rules,
such as ALWAYS swimming with a buddy, wearing a life jacket,
and only swimming under adult supervision.

WEATHER WORDS

Here are definitions to 100 weather words that help children become "Wise on Weather!" The definitions in **bold type** are from meteorologists. The other ones are from children who were asked what they thought these words meant. They are enlightening and entertaining (and sometimes correct). Enjoy!

Advisory: **A short-term forecast issued by the National Weather Service to caution about upcoming weather conditions.**
    A type of visor with ads on it.
    A person who gives advice.

Air: **The fluid that we breathe. (Yes, it really is a fluid.)**
    Something that cools you down.
    Something that gives us oxygen and helps us breathe.

Air Pressure: **The weight of the air on the earth, which means the difference between good and bad weather.**
    The amount of air in your bike tires.
    When air presses you.

Almanac: **Past weather facts.**
    Creatures that God made.
    Almonds that you eat that are very healthy for you.
    An almond that acts.
    Something you read.

Anemometer: **A weather instrument used to measure wind speed.**
    Someone who listens to monitors to find out about the weather.
    A colorful beanie with helicopter blades on top of it.
    Barometer and Thermometer's sister, Ann.

Atmosphere: **Where all the air is.**
    The space that surrounds the planet.
    When something's not fair.
    A big, huge meteor ball.

Aurora Borealis: **The Northern Lights.**
    A bowling alley.
    A roaring bologna sandwich.
    Something that cleans the planet.

Autumn: **The beginning of fall.**
    A girl's name.
    Another name for fall.
    When leaves fall off the trees.

Barometer: An instrument that measures air pressure.
    Thermometer's brother.
    Something that tells the temperature of the planet.

Blizzard: A really nasty storm in the winter.
    A big, huge snowstorm.
    My favorite dessert from Dairy Queen.

Breeze: Air in motion.
    Wind that moves.
    A little bit of wind.
    Blowing air.
    The Super Bowl MVP quarterback for the Saints.

Ceiling: The height of the lowest layer of clouds.
    The wall on top of the rooms in the house.
    What Dad says Mom is going to hit when we do something wrong.

Chilly: Uncomfortably cool or cold.
    The penguin Chilly Willy.
    Something yummy you eat during the fall that has beans in it.

Clear: Free of clouds, mist, or rain.
    What the doctor says before he puts the paddles on you to make you jump.
    Claire is the neighbor across the street.
    Not fuzzy.

Climate: Typical weather for a given area.
    The earth's temperature.
    Something you do when you climb a tree.
    You climb it to go into the playground.
    Unusual weather in a place.

Cloud: Moisture that is visible.
    Something that blocks the sun.
    White, fluffy things in the sky.
    Water droplets in the sky.
    Marshmallows in the sky.

Condensation: When moisture in the air turns to water.
    When you have a conversation.
    When your pop sits for a while and the outside of the glass gets wet.
    When you concentrate on weather.

Cool: A fairly low temperature.
    When you don't have a fever, you are as cool as a cucumber.
    Joe Cool from Snoopy.
    When you are popular in school.

Depression: A very weak storm in the Tropics.
    You put pressure on someone when they are hurt.
    When Mommy is sad.
    To push down with not a lot of pressure.

Dew: Water on the grass in the morning.
    A type of haircut.
    To do what your mom says.
    I'm a cool dude.
    A type of green pop that comes from a mountain.

Drizzle: Really, really, really tiny drops of rain.
    Something that blows leaves.
    What you do to put chocolate on ice cream.
    Little drops of rain.

Drought: Everything is dry.
    When it is drying up.
    No rain—dryness.

Earth: The ball on which we live.
    The only planet with oxygen.
    The planet we live on.
    Mother Earth.

El Niño: A warm water current in the Pacific Ocean that stirs weather patterns.
    A type of jalapeño pepper.
    Spanish word for Elmo.
    Spanish word for the fish Nemo.

Environment: The external conditions and surroundings where we all live.
    When you turn off lights to help the planet.
    The world around you.

Equator: The imaginary line around the earth that divides the northern and southern hemispheres.
    The dividing line.
    He might be related to Darth Vader.
    The world's belt.
    The waiter at the restaurant.

Fall: A transition season from warmer to cooler.
    When leaves fall off the trees and get ready for winter.
    The season after summer.
    Another word for autumn.
    When you wipe out on the ground and bump your head.

Flood: Too much water for the ground to keep up with.
    Water filling up the earth.
    The short pants my brother wears.
    A big, huge rainstorm that gets into your house and makes your house a swimming pool and full of water.

Fog: A cloud resting on the ground.
    A coat Mommy wears from London.
    A cloud on the ground.
    White stuff in the sky and you can't see anything.

Forecast: A prediction of what the weather will be.
    Something you do when fishing.
    When you put a coat on your forehead.
    Something a golfer with a broken arm yells.
    Another name for weather.
    When you cast a spell with the number four.
    Something that the weatherman does on the news.

Freeze: A period of frost or very cold.
    What happens to your brain when you slurp a frozen drink too fast.
    What the policeman says to the bad guy.
    A character in *Batman* and *The Incredibles*.

Front: A change of temperature coming.
    First in line.
    The opposite of back.

Frost: Frozen dew.
    I eat Frosted Flakes for breakfast.
    What you put on a cake, like frosting.
    Jack Frost.
    Little snow you get in the fall, but it's not snow. It's like ice on the ground.
    Something that freezes stuff like frosting on the grass.

Frostbite: Where your skin freezes.
    When you get really cold in the winter.
    When a piece of your skin gets so cold it dies.
    When Jack Frost bites your nose.
    Something that gets on you that freezes your thumb.

Funnel Cloud:
A really cool cloud that you don't want to get under.
- A dark cloud.
- A tornado that hasn't touched the ground yet.
- Something that's starting to turn into a tornado.
- Goes good with funnel cakes.
- A cotton candy machine.

Gale: A very strong wind on a lake or an ocean.
- When it's raining in the spring.
- A girl's name.
- A garden center up the street.

Glaze: Lots of ice.
- A fancy word for when stuff glows.
- Ice on the streets.
- A type of doughnut at doughnut Sunday.
- The look Mommy gives me when I do something bad.

Gust: Pretty good wind.
- Big winds.
- The mule who kicks the winning field goals.
- The mouse in *Cinderella* who is friends with Jack.

Hail: Ice cubes from the sky.
- When stuff is falling from the sky.
- Hard, hard, hard rain.
- "Hail to the Chief!"
- A prayer to Jesus' mommy: "Hail Mary, full of grace…"
- Two smidges harder than drizzle.

Haze: A very light fog.
- A hay maze.
- When you go on a hayride in the fall.
- When hay is blowing around in the fall.

Heat: Anything that feels warm.
- It's hot stuff.
- Something that is hot or really hot.
- A super-fast pitch in baseball.
- When a dog goes crazy.

Hemisphere: One side of the globe.
- When hail is falling and you don't have fear.
- Atmosphere's sister.
- Going to the fair.

Humidity: Moisture in the air.
- When there's a hot side and a cold side of the earth.
- Hot, sticky, and sweaty.
- The earth sweating.

Hurricane: A very windy tropical system.
- A tornado that happens in Florida.
- An earthquake underwater.
- A huge storm that starts in warm water.
- A big, huge wind that destroys stuff.
- His a cane.

Isobar: Squiggly line on a weather map.
- An ice cream bar.
- A type of candy.
- A bar with ice on it.

Jet Stream: Winds where the jets fly.
- Where the airplanes fly.
- When the jet flies so fast.
- A jet flying on a stream.

Lake Effect Snow: A snowstorm that plays favorites as to where it goes.
- Watery snow.
- Snow that the lake affects.
- Snow on a lake.
- Blizzards.

Lightning: A great spark of electricity.
  When light comes from the sky and knocks down trees.
  Electricity from the sky that can strike you down.
  Super fast like Lightning McQueen and the car in the movie *Grease*.
  A huge zap of a yellow laser and it shocks you.
  Pictures from heaven.

Meteorologist: Someone who studies weather.
  A person who studies meteors.
  A scientist.
  A weather-telling dude like Dick Goddard.
  Meteors coming from the sky.

Mist: Even smaller than drizzle.
  You missed a shot in the basketball game.
  Dew on the window.
  A harder rain than drizzle.
  A drink from the Sierras.

Monsoon: A seasonal wind.
  A French man.
  A monster.
  We'll see you soon on Monday.

Muggy: Summer humidity.
  When there's mud connected to mud.
  A mug of root beer.

Northern Lights: Energy from the sun hitting gases way up in the atmosphere, and energizing them and producing light.
  The lights that are on at a football game.
  Light coming in winter.
  Lights in the north.

Overcast: Cloudy.
  When something's flying over you.
  A cast of movie stars that stays to work over their shift.
  Something the weatherman does.
  When someone goes overboard off a ship.
  The part of your cast that your friends sign when you break your arm.

Precipitation: Rainy or snowy.
  It falls from the sky.
  When a priest sips from his cup.

Radar: How we can see rain.
  There's little dots of rain.
  It goes with Doppler.
  Something that the weatherman uses to see what's going on.
  A scanner that scans for rain and other stuff.
  What police used to give Mommy a speeding ticket.

Rain: Wet drops from the sky.
  Raindrops keep falling on my head.
  Water is falling from the sky.
  Earth's shower.
  Mist and drizzle together falling from the sky, and it gets you soaked.

Rainbow: Pretty colors from the sun and the rain.
  A flavor of Skittles candies.
  Beautiful colors that come after rain.
  Leads to a pot of gold.
  Mommy's nickname, Rambo.
  ROY G BIV (Red Orange Yellow Green Blue Indigo Violet).
  Something that comes from the sun and the rain and it's beautiful.

Ridge: A high pressure system that has been stretched like taffy.
    The road we take to get to Gramma's house.
    The bumps on my favorite type of potato chip.

Rime: Ice on mountaintops.
    When words have the same ending.
    Frosting on a mountain.

Rumble: Thunder.
    When clouds are crashing together.
    Rocks crushing together.
    To mumble when you talk.
    What wrestlers get ready to do.

Sandstorm: Wind that kicks up lots of sand.
    When it gets windy while you are at the beach.
    Sand blows all over the place.
    What happens in the desert.

Season: The year is divided into four seasons, and each one has its own weather patterns and daylight hours.
    There are four seasons in a year.
    What Daddy puts on the steak to make it taste yummy.
    I say "Merry Christmas!" instead of "Season's Greetings!"

Shadow: A dark area or shape produced by a body coming between rays of light and a surface.
    You are on the wall all gray.
    Something the groundhog sees on February 2nd.
    The reflection of you that the sunlight projects.
    Peter Pan lost his shadow.
    It follows you around.

Shower: Off and on rain.
    What I take because I don't like baths.
    A big, big rain.
    April showers bring May flowers.
    A party to get gifts when you are having a baby or getting married.

Sleet: Mini ice cubes.
    Falling ice.
    When you're tired and your eyes are shut.
    You take a long, long, rest and you snore real loud.

Slush: Partially melted ice or snow.
    Very cold frozen/chopped icy treat. I like blueberry.
    Soggy, soft snow.
    Mud or dirt mixed with water and grass.
    When there's a big puddle of stuff that slurps up.

Smog: Haze in the city.
    When smoke's going away.
    When there's not that much fog.
    Fog's brother.

Snow: Frozen rain.
    Little white cold things falling from the sky.
    Tons of snowflakes falling from the sky.
    Heaven's powdered sugar.

Snowflake: A frozen raindrop.
    Little diamonds of snow falling down.
    A pretty decoration we make from paper.
    A piece of snow and there are no two snowflakes the same.

Spring: **The change from cold to warm.**
>When flowers start to grow.
>The season after winter.
>To jump up like Tigger.
>Spring break, no school around Easter.
>The coils on the mattress that will pop out if you jump on the bed.

Squall: **A line of storms.**
>When lots of bugs are crawling on the ground.
>When there are small pieces of dead squirrels.
>An Indian princess.

Storm: **A powerful disturbance of the atmosphere with strong winds and often snow, rain, lightning or thunder.**
>Bad weather.
>When everything blows around.
>Lots and lots of rain.
>Weather that has a lot of snow, rain, or lightning where a lot of damage can happen.

Summer: **The hot season.**
>When the sun shines very hot.
>The season after spring.
>A girl's name.
>Summer never a bummer.

Sun: **What drives our weather.**
>A bright yellow ball of gas in the sky.
>Your girls are your daughters and your boys are your sons.
>A big, huge energy light that makes things hot.
>Superman gets his energy from this.

Sunburn: **Too much sun.**
>When you go out in hot weather and the sun burns your skin and turns it red.
>You get it from the sun and it hurts a lot so try not to get it.

Temperature: **The way we measure hot and cold.**
>You take this to tell if something is hot or cold.
>When your body temperature is not 98.6 degrees.
>Mercury in the thermometer.

Thermometer: **An instrument that tells the weather.**
>When there's a big camera in outer space that films down on earth.
>Something you stick under your tongue to see if you have a fever.
>Something that picks up radar.
>Pops out of a turkey when it is done cooking on Thanksgiving.
>An object that tells the temperature.

Thunder: **A sound that follows the spark from the sky.**
>A roar in the sky.
>Two clouds crashing together.
>Thunder from down under.
>Andre "Thunder" Thornton from the Cleveland Indians.
>The angels bowling in heaven and they get a strike.

Thunderstorm: **A big cloud that makes rain and loud noises.**
>Scary rain.
>A storm with thunder and lightning.

Tide: Water that moves up and down.
- It's when you tie your shoes.
- Alabama Crimson Tide.
- A song by Blondie called "The Tide Is High."
- A part to the ocean.
- What we use to wash our clothes.
- You tied the race if you both finished it at the same time.

Tornado: A small but nasty and dangerous wind.
- A really, really bad storm.
- It killed the Wicked Witch.
- Hot air and cold air mix together.
- Swirling wind.

Tornado Alley: Best place to see tornadoes.
- Where tornadoes go a lot.
- Where the tornadoes strike most and one of the states is Kansas.
- Where Uncle Mark bowls his perfect 300 games.

Tsunami: A giant, dangerous wave.
- Storms that just have thunder.
- A Sumo wrestling match.
- I eat this for my lunch instead of bologna or peanut butter.

Twister: A nickname for a tornado.
- A freaky whirlpool.
- A bad storm where everything blows around.
- Another name for a tornado.
- A type of dance Gramma Barbara likes to do.
- A fun game that twists your body into different positions on colored circles.

Typhoon: Same as a hurricane, but in a different place.
- It's where there are lots of animals.
- A type of cable used on a starship.
- When you type really fast.
- A big, giant wave.

Visibility: How far you can see.
- When you visit somebody with respect.
- Something that can turn you invisible or not invisible.
- The ability to be invisible and/or invincible.

Warning: A statement designed to help you get out of the way.
- When the weatherman warns you that there's going to be a tornado.
- What the police gives you if he doesn't give you a ticket after stopping you.
- My brother warns me he's going to chase me.

Watch: A statement designed to help you watch for weather.
- What Daddy does to the TV at night. He watches it.
- When you watch out to see if there's going to be a storm.
- Something you wear on your wrist to tell time.

Waterspout: A distant cousin to the tornado, but weaker.
- Where the itsy-bitsy spider went.
- The kids' TV station when it rains – PBS Sprout.
- A drinking fountain has a waterspout that you drink from.

Weather: It describes the condition of the air at a particular time.
> When people tell you if there's going to be a storm or not.
> Something that tells you what's going on outside.
> It's when God controls and thinks of what the day's going to look like outside.

Weatherman: A man who studies maps and predicts what the weather will be.
> He's on the news and tells us when we don't have school.
> Dick Goddard is the gold standard.
> He has a seal named AMS.
> Person who is always wrong about the weather.
> Somebody who tells you what the weather is going to be.

Weathervane: An instrument that points into the wind.
> There's a party outside and there's not nice weather.
> A vein to weather.
> A villain.
> The blue lines in your hand.

Whiteout: So much snow that you can't see.
> When the sky is all white.
> When there's a big storm of white snow everywhere and you can't see.
> The white stuff at school that covers up the mistakes you make with a pen.

Willy-Willy: Like a hurricane.
> A whale and its baby that want to be freed.
> When you lick your finger and stick it in someone's ear.
> Silly-silly.

Wind: Air that moves.
> It blows.
> The fast breeze that blows everything around.
> Something that makes the trees blow.

Wind Chill: How you feel when the wind blows in the winter.
> When it's chilly and windy.
> Chill out. We don't have school!

Windstorm: Anything that makes a wind.
> When wind blows everywhere with no thunder or lightning.
> A storm of just wind.
> A big, huge storm and winds all around it.

Winter: The cold season.
> When it's very, very cold outside and it snows a lot.
> The season after fall.
> When animals take a really long nap and hibernate.

Woollybear: A cute little fuzzy worm that predicts the weather.
> A big huge fall festival in Vermilion, Ohio.
> Related to teddy bear and gummy bear.
> A bear that people make warm sweaters out of when there are no sheep around.
> A caterpillar that tells us if we're going to have a rough or calm winter.
> Wooly Bully.